Fully Known
Fully Loved

A 30-Day Journey
of Your Identity
in Christ

A Flourishing in Faith Devotional

ELIZABETH RENICKS

TABLE OF CONTENTS

INTRODUCTION

"But to all who did receive him, who believed in his name, he gave the right to become children of God, who were born, not of blood nor of the will of the flesh nor of the will of man, but of God."
John 1:12-13 (ESV)

Sandwiched in the middle of the poetic first chapter of the Gospel of John is the powerful, life-altering fact described above. Everyone who receives Christ is given the right by God to become His child. This is the act of being born again that Jesus described to Nicodemus (John 3).

John 1:12 is the good news of the gospel in a nutshell. The outlines are simple: Receive Jesus. Believe in Him. In this, the Bible assures us, we are born again; we are able to enter into new life.

Being born into this new life grants us a host of blessings. It re-creates our identity. It reframes the whole narrative of our lives. The rest of Scripture frames and details this very basic truth, bringing to life for us the riches and benefits of being a child of the One True God.

So, why do we sometimes feel so unchanged? Like we have missed out on the freedom, the joy, and the abundant life Jesus came to bring to us?

It is all too easy, even for Christians, to live with the mindset of an orphan instead of the mindset of a beloved child of the King. An "orphan mindset" can look like living as though abandoned by God, rejected, forgotten, or overlooked by Him. It can look like living in a state of constant striving, trying to earn something that has been freely given. These are facets of an orphan mindset. I have walked in all of them at one time or another.

Part of an orphan mindset may have to do with the way we have come to view ourselves. We live in a world that conditions us to compare ourselves with others. Advertising campaigns sell us the idea that we are incomplete until we have purchased a new product. News headlines feed our fears and create dismay or distrust. Our minds can easily begin to be filled with negative self-talk, fear, and insecurity.

Living with an orphan mindset also comes about because living fully in our identity in Christ is regularly opposed. The enemy of God desires nothing more than to rip us away from trusting and experiencing God's love. A primary tactic Satan uses is to undermine our sense of the majestic identity we have as new creatures in Christ. Forces of darkness want us to live like orphans rather than as children of the King.

My prayer is that this devotional will help you lift your eyes to see yourself in a more grace-filled, generous light—the way God sees you. His Word is filled with encouragements and descriptions of your value to Him. The life, death, and resurrection of Jesus Christ put an end to the question of whether you hold value.

For the next month, you will be reminded of truths from Scripture about your identity. Through the power of the Holy Spirit living in you, these truths can remind, reshape, and restore you to embrace your identity as a beloved child of the King of the Universe.

Each day, you'll find a verse, a reflection, a question to consider, a prayer to pray, and an affirmation to proclaim about yourself. May your soul be strengthened, your heart be comforted, and your mind be transformed through the coming days of meditating on your identity in Jesus.

Begin with Foundations

You are dearly loved by the King of the Universe. He created you to live intimately with Him, to fellowship with Him, and to walk in fullness of life. When you commit to living as a follower of Christ, inviting Him to be your Lord, you become a child of God (John 1:12; Galatians 3:26). You have a rich identity as His beloved child. But the reality is, many things war against that identity.

To fully embrace your identity in Christ, it helps to remind yourself of the foundational truths about who you are and the world you inhabit.

These first seven entries are designed to help remind you of just that— simple but profound foundational truths about who you are and the shape of the story you are a part of. These foundational truths of our faith underpin your identity. We will start at the very beginning…not just your creation, but the creation of all things.

May you see more of the heart of the One who loves you dearly and deeply.

DAY 1
Imago Dei

"So God created man in His own image; in the image of God He created him; male and female He created them."
Genesis 1:27 (NKJV)

Several years ago, I was asked to make a list of the various roles and relationships I had at the time. I was stunned to discover I was trying to juggle more than twenty roles in at least ten different arenas. I had a lengthy list of "identities."

To my horror, I realized one item did not appear on my list: child of God. In the busyness of all those things, I had lost sight of the relationship that holds my key identity.

That got my attention.

How easily we can forget our origins. You might know the story of your birth or the story of your family and its history. These things can certainly shape your sense of identity.

But further back than that, you have a foundational identity: You were created by God. Not only were you created by God, but He created you **in His own image.** The Latin phrase historically used by the Church for this is *imago Dei*.

What does it mean that you are created in the image of God?

It means you are created in His likeness and in a way that reflects Him. Just as parents pass down their characteristics and traits to their children, God has given each of us some of His characteristics. Among them are creativity, the ability to reason, and the ability to form and sustain relationships with others.

Recognizing you are made in the image of God is significant. This truth highlights the inherent value you have as an image bearer of the creator and sustainer of all things. Before you ever put on any other sort of identity, you must begin with the profound truth of being made in the image of God. That is your starting point.

Reflect: What does the fact that you are made in God's image tell you about your value to Him?

Loving God, I receive the truth that my identity comes from You. Thank You for making me alive in You, and for making me in Your image. Help me remember today that I am Your image bearer.

God is the foundation of my identity; therefore, I am valuable and beloved.

DAY 2
Made with Purpose

"For we are God's masterpiece. He has created us anew in Christ Jesus, so we can do the good things he planned for us long ago."
Ephesians 2:10 (NLT)

You were made with purpose. Purpose is something we all long for.

One of the best-selling nonfiction books ever published is Rick Warren's 2002 release *The Purpose Driven Life*. It has sold more than fifty million copies in at least eighty-five languages.[1] Statistics like that testify to the fact that we all desire to have deep focus and meaning in our lives. We are hardwired for it.

In the beginning, God gave Adam and Eve specific roles and instructions. They had a mission and purpose. Having mission and purpose is one of the ways human beings are made *imago Dei*—in the image of God. The effects of the fall of man and sin have twisted up and marred everything about our sense of identity; even so, we still have God-given purpose.

Today's verse points to something profound and often misunderstood about God: He trusts you to be involved in His work. He joyously shares the rule over creation with you. He is not a distant, harsh taskmaster. Nor is He sitting on a lofty mountain, passively wanting to receive worship and praise from His created ones. No!

He is a "with-us" God! A God who invited and continually invites you to be with Him. This relationship and reality births deep purpose within you.

God delights in inviting you into leadership and influence in His world; He wants you to participate with Him in the creative work He is doing.

He does not *need* you to do anything for Him; He *allows* you to participate with Him. All have been designed with purpose, and we can only find our purpose and meaning in Him.

Reflect: How does knowing you are made with purpose impact you? Do you believe it?

Loving God, I receive the truth that I am made with purpose and that You have prepared specific things for me to do in this life. Bring this truth alive in my life today.

**God made me with a unique purpose,
and He is with me in living it out.**

DAY 3
Challenged by a Liar

"The serpent was the shrewdest of all the wild animals the LORD God had made. One day he asked the woman, 'Did God really say you must not eat the fruit from any of the trees in the garden?'"

Genesis 3:1 (NLT)

Unfortunately, the foundations of your identity repeatedly come under attack.

With Eve, Satan planted seeds of doubt about God and about who she believed herself to be. Before encountering the serpent, Eve trusted God for everything. She didn't doubt either His goodness or her own identity. With just a few questions, the serpent had her believing God was not trustworthy. He also had her believing she could become like a god herself.

Not much has changed. The enemy of your soul is still at work trying to challenge your faith in a loving, trustworthy God.

But Satan is a liar. Jesus called the devil "a liar and the father of lies" (John 8:44, ESV).

Our rational culture doesn't believe in a real devil who is active and destructive on earth. But Jesus did not think the devil was a cartoonish fantasy. Jesus took very seriously the reality and actions of His enemy.

All of Scripture testifies to this enemy of God who, from the beginning, has lied to deceive humanity.

Much in our world wages war against our God-given identity. Often the attacks are disguised as things that sound fairly good or seem to be "not such a big deal." Here's the problem: The temptations of the enemy all lead to independence from God instead of dependence on Him.

You would do well to consider the reality and impact of the father of lies, just as Jesus did. Walking in your identity in Christ includes recognizing the reality that you have an enemy who wants to destroy your confidence in God. You can rejoice that Jesus has defeated this enemy on the cross and made a way for you to experience freedom from his deceptions.

Reflect: Do you struggle to believe in the literal presence of God's enemy at work in our world? Why or why not?

Loving God, help me recognize the truth that my identity in You will come under attack. Give me eyes to see where I am being tempted to believe lies about who I am, instead of Your truth.

I will face opposition in living as a beloved child of God, but in Christ, I have victory over those challenges.

Delivered and Transferred

*"He has delivered us from the domain of darkness and transferred
us to the kingdom of his beloved Son, in whom we have
redemption, the forgiveness of sins."*
Colossians 1:13-14 (ESV)

This might be my favorite verse. It is certainly in my top five.

Our modern, scientifically oriented society does not make much room
for the realities of the supernatural realm. But that does not mean it
doesn't exist.

Some want to take a metaphorical approach to a verse like this, likening
the kingdom of darkness to something like the dark side of the Force
from *Star Wars*. They think of the supernatural as fantasy.

But the Bible makes it clear there is a real supernatural realm where a
real, ongoing battle occurs for the souls of human beings. While we
cannot always see the battle itself, we can certainly see the evidence of
it. The reality is of a supernatural domain of darkness where evil has
great power. Mere humans cannot, in their brokenness, hope to prevail
over it, no matter how many metaphorical lightsabers we try slinging
around.

That victory is the work of Jesus and His resurrection. He triumphed
over the powers of darkness.

When you met Jesus and received His grace and forgiveness into your life, you were transferred out of the realm where darkness and sin prevail. Darkness is now no longer the domain you live in. Your citizenship has been transferred. Your home address is the kingdom of the Son of God, who gave His life for you.

If you want to get really excited about what this means, spend time meditating on who Jesus is by reading Colossians 1:15-20. Or read through the first couple of chapters of Ephesians. Digging deep into these passages reveals the glory of the kingdom into which believers in Christ have been transferred.

Being rescued from the domain of darkness is a really big deal. May you have the grace to receive this gift.

Reflect: What ways can you see the forces of darkness at work around you? How have you seen Jesus overcome those dark forces?

Loving God, I receive the truth that I belong to the kingdom of Jesus Christ. Help me to see with spiritual eyes the blessings and reality of this truth today.

As a Christian, I no longer live in the domain of darkness. Christ has transferred me into the realm of light.

DAY 5
Debt Free

"He erased the certificate of debt, with its obligations, that was against us and opposed to us, and has taken it away by nailing it to the cross."

Colossians 2:14 (CSB)

Have you ever had a person pay a bill for you or buy you a meal at a restaurant? What about experiencing forgiveness from someone who has accused you or been angry with you? A burst of freedom and joy comes in response to being released from obligation or accusation.

Imagine that grace and blessing on the largest possible scale, with the most impossible debt being erased. That is what believers have in Christ. Can you even begin to grasp the magnitude of the sin and enslavement you have been released from?

The word here translated "certificate of debt" is used only this one time in the Bible. The word in the Greek is *cheirographon,* which means "something handwritten."[2] This word was used in financial contexts, such as a handwritten IOU. Some scholars, however, interpret the phrase "certificate of debt" as a legal reference to the Law of Moses.

Whether in the financial realm or the legal realm, this verse affirms that no charge can stand against us. Jesus took away *all* the charges and debts of our sin and nailed them to the cross. It can be helpful to consider both the legal and financial perspectives.

When you hear condemning voices of accusation bringing charges against you, lean into the legal imagery of this verse. All accusations and charges against you have been dropped in the courts of God. You are free.

If you fall prey to messages telling you to work harder to earn God's favor or acceptance, lean into the financial imagery of this verse. All of the costs of your sin and brokenness have been erased, fully paid, borne by Jesus. All of them. You are released from debt.

You can live debt free with regard to all the charges of sin against you. What a gift! This is another foundation of your true identity in Christ. May you receive and walk in this truth today.

Reflect: What sorts of condemning or accusing messages come against you?

Loving God, I receive the truth that, at the cross, You have canceled all the charges against me. Bring this truth alive in my life today.

Jesus has erased all my debts.
I am debt free in God's eyes.

DAY 6
New in Christ

"Therefore, if anyone is in Christ, he is a new creation; the old has passed away, and see, the new has come!"
2 Corinthians 5:17 (CSB)

Do you know the feeling of having a new pair of shoes that needs "breaking in" before they begin to feel comfortable? At first, you may only be able to wear the new pair for a brief time before your feet start urging you to slip back into a more comfortable, old pair. It takes a little while before the new shoes feel as good as the old ones.

That sensation is what it can feel like to embrace the truth that you have a new identity in Christ. It might feel like a struggle to walk in the "new shoes" of new life. It might even seem that some of the old shoe, old life habits are more comfortable or familiar.

Maybe you do not always feel like the new creation you are in Christ. Maybe this truth has not come into your daily life in a meaningful way. Psychologists have studied the limitations of our perceptions when it comes to reality. A gap exists. A common example is the limitations of human perception of color and sound. Just because you cannot hear a sound at the frequency of a dog whistle does not mean a dog whistle isn't a real thing.

It is the same with experiencing the fullness of new life in Christ. Like breaking in a new pair of shoes, you must recognize the journey of learning to inhabit the truth of your new identity in Christ. As the perception-reality gap shows, you must also realize truth is true even if you can't always feel it.

Scripture reminds you to walk by faith, not by sight. You are a new creature in Christ. May you have patience with yourself and recognize God's grace to you as you walk with Him, breaking in your new-life shoes and discovering your full, redeemed identity in Christ.

Reflect: In what ways do you struggle to experience the reality that you are a new creation in Christ?

Loving God, I receive the truth that I have a new identity in Christ. Give me grace as I grow in embracing this truth. Help me today to break in my "new-life shoes" a little more.

Christ has made me new, and I can learn to walk in that newness with His faithful care.

DAY 7
Perfected in Faith

"Let us fix our eyes on Jesus, the author
and perfecter of our faith…"
Hebrews 12:2a (NIV 1984)

A lot of theology is packed into the seven-word description of Jesus in this verse. This 1984 NIV is the version I memorized as a young believer, and I love the clear depiction here of what Jesus does for us.

He authors your faith. He perfects your faith. These are powerful truths.

Other translations describe Jesus as the initiator, originator, pioneer, or champion of your faith. He is also the One who gets you and your faith across the finish line. The Good News Translation puts it beautifully: Jesus is the One "on whom our faith depends from beginning to end" (Hebrews 12:2a, GNT).

This is incredibly good news! This gift is the heart of your new identity in Christ. The faith upon which your daily new life in Christ rests is a gift from Him from start to finish.

But oh, how hard it can be for us to rest in this truth at times. We are busy. We are overwhelmed. We are deceived into thinking everything rests on our own shoulders.

In the press of day-to-day life, you can look to Jesus. More than that, you are urged by this verse to *fix* your eyes on Him. This is more than a passing glance. It is dialed in, laser locked, and utterly reliant.

This verse reminds you that you are never on your own.

Jesus birthed your faith journey; He perfects your faith and brings it to fullness and completion. The Bible tells you that Jesus will be faithful to complete what He has begun in you (Philippians 1:6). What good news, and what a solid foundation for walking in your identity in Him.

Reflect: What difference does it make to realize that Jesus is the One who begins and completes your faith?

Loving God, I receive the truth that You are the author and finisher of my faith. Help me today to keep my eyes fixed on You and to experience Your nearness.

I am not alone walking out my faith. Jesus begins and completes it. I can rely on His faithfulness to grow me into what He has planned for me.

SECTION TWO
Embrace Your Identity in Christ

When you become a follower of Christ, you get a whole new identity. Gone is the "old man" who was enslaved to sin and enmeshed in fear. "…[T]he new has come!" declares 2 Corinthians 5:17 (CSB). We live this new life "by faith in the Son of God" (Galatians 2:20, ESV).

Sadly, it can be hard in our broken world to remember what that newness looks like. So, for the next fourteen entries, you will be meditating on words and thoughts centered around your identity in Christ.

Each entry in this section centers on one adjective that describes the truth of who you are as a child of God. As you come to each entry, invite the Holy Spirit to guide you into truth and into surrender, especially if it is a description that you struggle to believe applies to you.

May you come to know more and more about your identity in Christ, so you can develop increased "beloved-child thinking" about yourself and your life.

DAY 8
Alive

"So, you too consider yourselves dead to sin and alive to God in Christ Jesus."

Romans 6:11 (CSB)

Many Christians long for a deeper experience of God but feel stuck or dulled to the possibility of growth. Perhaps you identify with that.

At times, you can be so worn down by your daily life that it is hard to recognize the glory of being fully alive. Jesus talked of coming so you could have *life* and have it "in the fullest possible way" (John 10:10, NIRV). He gives you the gift of being fully alive.

This aliveness is more than simply trudging through your days, "working for the weekend." It is a vital and animated existence, rooted in the very Author of Life Himself.

If you belong to Christ, you are alive in this very full and dynamic way. You may not always feel like it or realize it. You may feel worn down and weary in ways that seem the complete opposite of vitality and aliveness to God. But remember, your feelings don't change facts.

Paul recognized the power feelings can have when he penned this verse in Romans. Notice the word *consider* found in today's verse. (In other translations, this word is rendered *count* or *reckon*.) Today's verse says you are to consider yourself "alive to God in Christ Jesus." We have a choice concerning the dulling power of sin.

As God's child, you must consider yourself as you truly are in Christ: alive to God. The power of sin tempts you to consider yourself otherwise. Romans 6:11 reminds you that, in Christ, you are truly alive. If that is not your current experience, perhaps this is a place to begin in prayer. Ask God to give you a sense of the full, dynamic aliveness to Him that Christ purchased for you on the cross. Ask Him to help you walk in this part of your identity.

Reflect: Do you feel alive to God or more dulled or stuck in relation to Him? What causes those feelings?

Loving God, I receive the truth that I am fully alive in Christ and that I can consider myself dead to those things that want to dull my sense of vitality in relation to God. Help me to walk in this truth today.

I can choose to believe I am alive in Christ and dead to any sin that tries to dull my life in Him.

DAY 9
Blameless

"He will also strengthen you to the end, so that you will be
blameless in the day of our Lord Jesus Christ."
1 Corinthians 1:8 (CSB)

According to the *Oxford English Dictionary,* to be blameless means "to be innocent of wrongdoing."[3]

This is an astounding thought: You are considered innocent of any wrongdoing before God's throne. If I'm honest, I can barely get a foot out of bed in the morning before I am wronging someone with unbidden, condemning thoughts. Usually, the target is me.

Perhaps you can relate. So, how can we be blameless? Only because of Jesus. Colossians 1:22 says Jesus reconciles believers to God through His death, presenting us "holy and blameless and above reproach" before the Father (ESV).

The Greek word used for *blameless* in both today's verse and in Colossians 1:22 takes the concept a step further than the *Oxford English Dictionary.* According to *Thayer's Greek Lexicon,* it means one who "cannot be called to account, unreprovable, unaccused, blameless."[4]

My experience is often contrary to that. I am rather good at reproving or scolding myself regularly. I feel the brunt of accusation and blame from voices around me and in my own head. We all have an inner critic who likes to accuse us of failure and wrongdoing, who likes to catalog all our imperfections and sins.

Are you familiar with this inner critic who starts hurling accusations at you before you've had your morning coffee? According to Scripture, you do not have to listen to those accusations because in God's eyes, you are unaccused.

If you are in Christ, you are blameless before God. It can be tempting to be hard on yourself, to live in a grip of shame. Your identity in Christ is different from blame and shame. It is blameless.

Embrace your blamelessness today. Be a little less hard on yourself. Remind yourself that, in Christ, you are beyond accusation. Ask the Holy Spirit to help you live in that identity more and more.

Reflect: What areas of blame or self-condemnation do you wrestle with the most?

Loving God, I receive the truth that I am blameless before God, and that there is no condemnation for me. Bring this truth alive in my life today.

In Christ, I am blameless before God.
I can reject condemnation.

DAY 10
Beloved

"Therefore be imitators of God, as beloved children."
Ephesians 5:1 (ESV)

In Christ, you are a beloved child of God. Stop right now and say to yourself: "I am a beloved child of God. I am deeply loved. I am beloved."

The need to be loved is not simply a teaching of Christianity. Even those who laugh in the face of the idea of a loving, personal God would acknowledge a core drive of humanity is to be affirmed, to be loved, and to know that we are "okay." This truth has been the subject of scientific studies. It has been affirmed by writers and storytellers for centuries.

Everyone you ever meet wants to be loved. Deeply loved. Much loved. Beloved. God wants you to know how deeply you are loved. Personally and intimately loved.

"But how do I know I am beloved?" you might ask. The answer cannot be found just in the evidence of your emotions. They will change with the circumstances, and they will not always speak truth to you. The answer lies in the gospel.

God shows us His love in that "while we were still sinners, Christ died for us" (Romans 5:8 ESV). We can know we are beloved because God sent His only Son to offer us a way of escape from sin and death (John 3:16-17).

Has the gospel become so familiar to you that you have lost sight of how stunning a thing it is for Jesus to have died for you? As Paul reminds us in Romans 5:7, it is pretty rare for a person to die for even a righteous person. Jesus came for you. You are His beloved, and He delights in you.

Lift your eyes up to see and receive the deep belovedness you have as God's child in Christ. He is longing for you. He delights in you. You are beloved.

Reflect: Do you have trouble viewing yourself as beloved by God? If so, why?

Loving God, help me to remember and to receive the astonishing truths of the gospel that affirm I am beloved by You. Help me to understand more of the depth of Your love for me. Bring this truth alive in me today.

I am God's beloved. He delights in me.

DAY 11
Included

*"And you also were included in Christ when you heard the
message of truth, the gospel of your salvation. When you believed,
you were marked in him with a seal, the promised Holy Spirit."*
Ephesians 1:13 (NIV)

The opposite of *included* is *excluded*. Being excluded can be a painful,
life-shaping experience. Being included can be a delightful, life-giving
experience.

Being included in Christ is a blessed, eternity-altering experience.

If you have received Christ, the good news is that you are included. In
Christ, your identity has shifted from outsider to insider. The original
context of this verse was that of the divide between Gentiles and Jews.
Paul's writing in Ephesians explains God's plans to welcome previously
excluded Gentiles into His covenant promises to Israel (Ephesians
2:11-22). God is an inclusive God.

This inclusion is all about union, a drawing together of things that had
previously been vastly divided and separated, like our sin once
separated us from God.

If you have placed your faith in Christ, according to our verse, you
have been given the Holy Spirit as a mark of belonging. This is a
mysterious union of supernatural proportions. If you are in Christ, the

Living God dwells within you. This is eternal, everlasting inclusion, not subject to the whims of circumstances or the hurtful actions of others.

Your inclusion in Christ also changes your citizenship. You become a citizen of God's kingdom, among His chosen people, a beneficiary of His ancient covenant promises to Israel. You are united to other believers within the body of Christ. The New Testament has much to say about the supernatural interconnected reality of God's family.

When you are in Christ, you are never excluded. You are never alone. You are never an outsider. Plenty of things will try to make you feel excluded in this world. In Christ, you can reject all of them. Walk in your identity. You are included.

Reflect: How often do you feel excluded or alone? What contributes to this?

Loving God, I receive the truth that I am included. When my feelings or circumstances make me forget this truth, bring it alive in my heart.

I am never alone because Christ includes me. When I feel alone, I can cry out to God to remind me I am included.

DAY 12
Child

"So in Christ Jesus you are all children of God through faith."
Galatians 3:26 (NIV)

According to today's verse, you become a child of God through faith in Christ. Being a "child of God" is one of those phrases that gets tossed around in Christian culture without much thought. But it is a big deal.

Part of your identity in Christ is as royalty in the most powerful ruling family of all time. There is not a higher King than the Lord God, the Holy One of Israel. All of the Bible attests to this fact.

But living as royalty—especially as a child of the One True King—can be a challenging thing to assimilate into your identity. The Bible is full of examples of God's children forgetting they have a loving, heavenly Father who would meet their needs.

The world doesn't make embracing your identity as a beloved child in God's family any easier. Many, many things war against a Christian who seeks to live fully in the identity of beloved child of the Most High King.

Two verses can encourage you to recall who you are. Romans 8:16 tells you the Holy Spirit bears witness to your status as God's child. As a Christian, you can quiet your soul and listen to the truth the Holy Spirit speaks to you deep within: You belong to Him.

Hebrews 12:2 exhorts you to fix your eyes on Christ. This verse speaks of Christ's enduring the cross and ascending victoriously over sin and death, finally being seated at the right hand of the throne of God. He did all that for you, so you could be His child. Children in healthy families are carefree, trusting, and joyous. They know their family delights in them.

God is the perfect parent, head of the most royal family in the Universe. Part of your identity in Christ is the carefree, joyous childlikeness of knowing you are a part of His family.

Reflect: Do you ever long to be a child again? Do you have a sense of childlikeness in relation to God?

Loving God, I receive the truth that I am Your child. May I be joyous, carefree, and confident of my place in Your family today.

I am a child of God, which means I belong to the most royal ruling family of all time.

DAY 13
Clothed

"I am overwhelmed with joy in the LORD my God! For he has dressed me with the clothing of salvation and draped me in a robe of righteousness."

Isaiah 61:10 (NLT)

I was talking to a friend once about laundry. It was in the context of a larger conversation about waiting on the Lord and learning to discern His voice. But the subject of our mundane, day-in-day-out activities came up.

The fact is, on this earthly plane, we do laundry. We have to think about clothes, keeping them clean, making sure they fit, making sure they are not stained. Some people may think more than others do about whether their clothes are currently in fashion, but we do have to wear something.

In the heavenly realms, however, we do not have to think about clothes because Christ followers are already clothed royally, according to Isaiah 61. This is in part a metaphor, of course. I don't have any idea what we will wear in heaven.

But I do know that right now, both on earth and in the heavenly realm where believers are already seated with Christ (Ephesians 2:6), we are covered and clothed in Christ. As today's verse says, we are dressed in salvation and draped in a robe of righteousness.

In other words, you have an identity in Christ. That means you are covered in His righteousness. When Adam and Eve sinned and their eyes were opened to knowing evil, the first thing that assaulted them was shame over nakedness (Genesis 3:7). We have been battling the monster of shame ever since. What Jesus does for you and for me is take away our nakedness and our shame before God. He dresses us royally.

Here's some bad news: Until Jesus comes back, you are still going to have to do laundry here on earth.

Here's some good news: God has robed you royally in the supernatural realm. Shame cannot destroy those garments. They are perfect, no laundry required. That glorious identity is a pure gift!

Reflect: What sorts of circumstances make you feel exposed, naked, or ashamed?

Loving God, I receive the truth that You have clothed me in righteousness. Because of this, I can be free from shame. Help me walk in the truth of being clothed in Christ today.

I am clothed in royal robes of righteousness. I can reject accusations and shame because of what Jesus has done for me.

DAY 14
Chosen

"Even before he made the world, God loved us and chose us in Christ to be holy and without fault in his eyes."

Ephesians 1:4 (NLT)

Do you remember what it was like on the playground when it was time to divide up into teams? Unless you were the kid who always got to be captain or the kid who always knew you would be picked first, you probably experienced at least a few moments of panic about being picked last. Even middle-of-the-packers could not be one hundred percent sure.

I can recall that sinking feeling in the pit of my stomach. Racing heartbeat. Fidgeting. Facial expressions toggling between pretended nonchalance and pleading eyes directed at the captains. I can sometimes still feel the waves of elementary school insecurity. I had a lot of it on the playground.

It can be isolating and confidence-shaking when we are not chosen.

Maybe you don't identify with the group games scenario. I am willing to bet you have another experience of feeling the anxiety of not being chosen. It stalks us all in one way or another.

Here is good news about your identity in Christ. You are chosen.

According to our verse today, you aren't simply chosen, but God loved you and chose you before He made the world. That is astonishing. Before He said, "Let there be light," He thought of you. He not only thought of you but chose you to be blameless in His eyes. The most important team captain of all time has selected you for Himself.

Allow the reality of Christ choosing you to wash over you today. Let it wash away all the scars and wounds of not being chosen in your past—on the playground or elsewhere. Exhale and release all the insecurity. Breathe in the delight of being selected, seen, known, and delighted in. He sees you. He chooses you.

Reflect: What are ways you have experienced feeling unchosen or rejected? Have you ever invited God to show you His perspective or His presence at those times?

Loving God, I receive the truth that You choose me. You have picked me for Your family. Bring this truth alive in my life today.

I am chosen by God. He sees me, and He chooses me.

Restored

*"The LORD is my shepherd; I shall not want. He makes me lie
down in green pastures. He leads me beside still waters. He
restores my soul."*

Psalm 23:1-2 (ESV)

We all have a deep need for times of refreshing and reset. It is one of
the reasons we plan vacations or retreats. Our lives can be so busy and
chaotic that we long for times of "getting away from it all." We need
things that restore us to energy.

But it goes much deeper than that.

Restoration of your soul is very much a part of the daily rhythm of
relationship with God. It is also very much a part of your identity in
Christ.

In Christ, you are restored to fellowship with God. But your soul is
also being restored again and again in defense against the ravages of the
fallen world around us. As with any restoration project, the restoration
of your soul is a process that takes time. Part of the restoration process
is rest. Lying down in green pastures; being led to still waters.

Stepping back, taking time away from the normal routines and hustle
and bustle is built into the fabric of God's created order. He ordained a
Sabbath at the very point of creation. Jesus repeatedly modeled
withdrawing from His ministry.

This stepping back for restoration is countercultural in a world that tells you to produce, perform, be perfect, be present, and on and on. Today, rest in your identity as one Christ has restored. Ask the Lord to help you confidently take steps to resist the blare of the world so you can live in the restoration and rest that is yours in Christ.

It makes a difference that we embrace our restoration in Christ. Whatever the magnitude of restoration your soul requires, know that Jesus knows all about it. He knows exactly what you need.

Reflect: What in your soul right now is most in need of restoration?

Loving God, thank You that, in Christ, I am restored to fellowship with You. May I pay attention to the need for deep restoration of my soul that comes in daily relationship with Jesus.

In Christ, I am restored to God, and He is restoring all the worn-out things in my soul.

DAY 16
Rescued

"I sought the LORD, and he answered me and rescued me from all my fears."

Psalm 34:4 (CSB)

God is a rescuer. Passages throughout the Bible tell of God's rescue of His children.

Today's verse mentions God rescuing from all fears. Other passages mention God rescuing His children from strong enemies and haters (Psalm 18:17); strife with people (Psalm 18:43); troubles (Psalm 91:15); distress (Psalm 107:6); tears (Psalm 116:8); stumbling (Jude 1:24); traps (Psalm 91:3); and death (Psalm 68:20).

If nothing on that list resonates with you, Psalm 34:19 (CSB) asserts the righteous have "many adversities," but the Lord rescues from all of them. Everything. Every single snare or trap.

In other words, as a child of God, you have been rescued from many things, big and small. Do you regularly consider, as part of your identity, the fact that you are rescued?

Have you ever gotten stuck in a place of overwhelm to the point you believed no help was coming? At those times, it is critical to remind yourself that, in Christ, you have been rescued for all time. Today, embrace the reality that God has already rescued you, God is continually rescuing you, and God will always rescue you.

The most significant thing Christ has rescued you from is the power of sin. Recall from Day 4 that Jesus has rescued His saints "from the domain of darkness and transferred us to the kingdom of his beloved Son" (Colossians 1:13, ESV). Through Jesus you have forgiveness of sins. You have been rescued from your biggest problem.

You can remind yourself of all Christ rescues you from by spending time in His Word, meditating on what He has done for you. Knowing the truth about all the ways you are rescued makes you more secure in this great facet of your identity in Christ.

May you experience the reality of God's rescue in your life today.

Reflect: Do you live more as one who is rescued or as one mired in troubles, longing for rescue?

Loving God, I receive the truth that, in Christ, I have been rescued from every power that seeks to destroy me or my relationship with You. Bring this truth alive in my life today.

I have been rescued by a responsive and loving God. He releases me from all snares.

DAY 17
Redeemed

"In him we have redemption through his blood, the forgiveness of our trespasses, according to the riches of his grace."
Ephesians 1:7 (ESV)

Most of us are familiar with the word *redeem* in the context of credit card rewards or frequent flier miles. Those of a "certain age" might even remember redeeming Green Stamps. If you remember that, you might also recall singing a Fanny Crosby hymn with the lyric: "Redeemed, how I love to proclaim it."

The Greek word translated *redemption* in Ephesians 1:7 is *apolytrōsis,* which means "a releasing effected by payment of ransom," according to *Blue Letter Bible.*[5] To be redeemed is to be bought back. One of the most accessible pictures of this in our day is that of a kidnapping or hostage situation. Hostages are released once a payment or exchange has been negotiated. Often the payment is expensive, and negotiations are complex.

If you belong to Jesus, you are redeemed from all sin. Your redemption was also expensive and complex. It came at the incredible cost of Christ's incarnation, crucifixion, death, and resurrection. Modern hostage negotiations go to great lengths to avoid the shedding of blood. Our eternal, spiritual redemption could only have come with the spilling of Christ's blood. Yours was the most extravagant and expensive ransom in all of history.

This precious redemption is a part of the fabric of your identity in Christ. You have been freed from all sin. All charges against you. You have been freed from the bondages of worry, deadlines, stress, uncertainty, and all other snares trying to take you hostage. You may have a chorus of inner critics telling you to work harder, do better, or be better. Those are lying voices that stand opposed to the truth of your identity in Christ as proclaimed by Scripture: You are fully redeemed by the blood of the Lord Jesus.

You can declare with the lyrics of Fanny Crosby's hymn: "Redeemed, how I love to proclaim it. Redeemed by the blood of the Lamb. Redeemed through His infinite mercy. His child, and forever, I am."[6]

Reflect: Do you ever feel like you have been "taken hostage" by anything? How does the truth that Christ has fully redeemed you affect that feeling?

Loving God, I receive the truth that Christ has fully redeemed me. When I feel taken hostage by worries, tasks, or pressures, remind me of the reality of my redemption.

I am redeemed. Jesus Christ has paid the ransom for all things attempting to take me hostage.

DAY 18
Seen

"So she called the name of the LORD who spoke to her, 'You are a God of seeing,' for she said, 'Truly here I have seen him who looks after me.'"
Genesis 16:13 (ESV)

Today's word, *seen,* is connected to one of my favorite names for God, which is the Hebrew *El-Roi,* meaning "a God who sees."

This God-naming came from Hagar, the servant of Sarai, wife of Abram. Hagar fled from Sarai after an ill-advised scheme to provide Abram with an heir. You can read all about it in Genesis 16. Suffice it to say, Hagar had a lot of relational brokenness, fear, and confusion in her life.

God saw Hagar in the midst of her running away and her wilderness experience. She encountered Him at one of the lowest points of her life and discovered God to be "him who looks after me" (Genesis 16:13, ESV).

As an Egyptian slave woman living in the household of Abram, Hagar was by no stretch of the imagination what today we would call a Christian, or even an observant Jew. And yet, God met her in the midst of deep trial. She was seen.

Hagar's story tells us something fundamental about who God is—a God of compassion and mercy (Exodus 34:6). It also reveals God's common grace, a theological term used to describe God's goodness to all of humanity, to encourage those who do not yet know Him to turn to Him and find life. Jesus spoke of this common grace during the Sermon on the Mount, saying God, "makes his sun rise on the evil and on the good, and sends rain on the just and on the unjust" (Matthew 5:45, ESV).

Regardless of your circumstances, you can be deeply comforted that you are seen by the compassionate and merciful God of the Universe. You may not understand how you merit that attentiveness, but you can believe it. You are seen by the One who looked so tenderly at Hagar.

May you experience His loving gaze as well today.

Reflect: Would you say you feel more seen or unseen by God? Why?

Loving God, thank You that You see me, regardless of whether it seems true to me or not. Strengthen my ability to sense Your loving gaze upon me today.

I am seen by the great, merciful, and compassionate God who created all things.

DAY 19
Known

"I am the good shepherd. I know my own and my own know me,
just as the Father knows me and I know the Father."
John 10:14-15a (ESV)

The words of John 10 are a rich and beautiful part of the Bible's record of Jesus' life on earth. Echoing the beloved imagery of Psalm 23, Jesus here uses an extended metaphor in which He identifies Himself as a good shepherd taking care of a flock of beloved sheep.

John 10 records Jesus describing the way a shepherd leads his sheep, calling each one by name. He goes on to contrast a true shepherd with a thief or a hired hand. The ultimate proof of a shepherd's devotion to his flock, Jesus says, is the willingness to sacrifice his life for the sheep.

All of this is remarkable. What a beautiful metaphor of care Jesus expresses throughout the first half of this chapter. But it gets even better in today's verses, where Jesus describes what is true about how deeply His followers are known by Him.

Jesus' followers and disciples are known in a shockingly intimate way. He says He knows us "just as the Father knows me." You would not question that God the Father knows Jesus inside and out. But how readily do you embrace that Jesus knows you just as intimately?

More so, Jesus goes on to say that you can know Him in the same way He knows the Father. John 10:14-15a says you can know Jesus in a deeply familial, intimate, trusting, and entwined way.

Think about that for a minute. It is mind-blowing in the best way possible. This sort of being known is a depth of relationship that is beyond description.

What a great grace to be known intimately by Him and to be confident that we can know God intimately as well.

Reflect: How does it make you feel to know you are fully known by God?

Loving God, I receive the truth that You fully know me. When I feel isolated or overlooked, help me embrace You as the tender of my heart. Help me realize how fully known I am by You today.

I am fully known by a compassionate and merciful God who loves me.

DAY 20
Accepted

"…to the praise of the glory of His grace, by which He made us accepted in the Beloved."

Ephesians 1:6 (NKJV)

You are accepted in Christ. Let that just wash over you for a minute.

I spent a good bit of my childhood feeling unaccepted and unsure of where I fit in. I attended four different elementary schools over five years. I was perpetually the new kid. It was often hard to feel accepted.

You probably have experience with this; haven't you had times of insecurity, wondering if you are accepted or where you fit in? I know how it stings when you don't feel accepted. Jesus does too.

He knows rejection in ways that make my elementary school days seem like ridiculously small potatoes. And yet, He cared enough about my small potatoes and my hurting heart to pay an unthinkable price. He paid that price for the hurts in your heart, too. He cares so much for you.

He has made a way to assure you that you are accepted. Always. No matter what.

The word translated *accepted* in Ephesians 1:6 is a Greek word used only two times in the Bible. Here it describes us as an accepted part of God's beloved.

The other time it is used? In Luke 1:28, when an angel greets Mary, the future mother of Jesus, describing her as "highly favored." Both *accepted* in Ephesians 1:6 and *highly favored* in Luke are expressions the Greek word *charitoō*[7].

Just as Mary was called highly favored, in Christ, you have been "honored with blessings, compassed with favor, or pursued with grace" as the word *charitoō* means. This is a deep acceptance.

Mary doubtless experienced times of feeling utterly rejected or misunderstood. But that doesn't change the fact that in God's sight, she was highly favored. You, too, may experience times of wondering if you are truly accepted. Those times do not change the reality of your acceptance. This favor is part of your identity in Christ.

Reflect: What experiences make you feel rejected? What makes you feel accepted?

Loving God, I receive the truth that I am accepted, especially when this world tries to make me feel rejected. Bring this truth alive in my life today.

Regardless of my circumstances, I am accepted—highly favored—by Christ at all times.

Friend

"I no longer call you servants, because a servant does not know his master's business. Instead, I have called you friends, for everything that I learned from my Father I have made known to you."
John 15:15 (NIV)

For some, the idea of friendship with God feels too "familiar" or even dishonoring to His majesty and holiness. For others, it seems an unattainable goal to have a comfortable, conversational, side-by-side relationship with God similar to what one has with a close, trusted, earthly friend.

Yet the Bible affirms God's desire to relate to you with exactly that sort of intimacy.

Long before Jesus declared His friendship to the disciples in John 15:15, God went to great lengths to create ways for human beings to engage with Him in intimate ways. The Lord considered Abraham a confidant who could be trusted with His plans (Genesis 18:18); Abraham is later described as a friend of God (James 2:23).

Throughout the Old Testament, God continually offered invitations to His children to rest in trusting relationship with Him, and He made ways through the law to come nearer to Him.

Then, the incarnation of Christ made a better way—God with us, Immanuel. He came to us in the flesh. Finally, at Jesus' ascension, the

Holy Spirit came to dwell within the children of God. That is "God with us" at a whole new level. Certainly, a willingness to live within you is an indication of God's willingness to engage you in the way Jesus describes in John 15:15.

God is forever wooing us, inviting us into friendship with Himself. We can reject that idea, or refuse the idea, but the truth remains that He is (and always has been) pursuing our hearts.

If you have given your life to Jesus, a part of your identity is that you are a friend of God. You can have confidence "to enter the holy places by the blood of Jesus" (Hebrews 10:19, ESV). He has made a way for you to enjoy a deep and comfortable friendship with the creator of all things.

In an era of unprecedented levels of loneliness, it is all the more significant to embrace the truth that God delights in you as His friend. May you pursue friendship with Him in confidence and joy.

Reflect: What are the characteristics you most look for in a friend?

Loving God, help me to experience the joys of friendship with You. In times when I struggle with loneliness or isolation, help me to know satisfying heart-to-heart fellowship with You.

I am a friend of God. I can have an intimate relationship with Him.

Live Out Who You Are in Christ

The journey of learning to walk in your identity as Christ's beloved is a lifelong endeavor. Paul writes of this in Philippians 3:12-14 (NLT):

> *I don't mean to say that I have already achieved these things or that I have already reached perfection. But I press on to possess that perfection for which Christ Jesus first possessed me. No, dear brothers and sisters, I have not achieved it, but I focus on this one thing: Forgetting the past and looking forward to what lies ahead, I press on to reach the end of the race and receive the heavenly prize for which God, through Christ Jesus, is calling us.*

This giant of the Christian faith had been following Christ for almost thirty years when he penned these words. Yet Paul still longed for spiritual growth and the full perfection that will come only when we see Jesus face to face. This speaks grace to us! We are called to press on with our eyes on Christ.

The next entries focus on the characteristics of those whose lives are lived in an identity founded in Jesus. Each entry is titled with a statement describing what your life can be when your identity is rooted in Christ. Each of these statements represents attitudes and outlooks based on truth. These perspectives can create deep stability within you because they remind you that Jesus brings you these things as gifts of identity in Him.

The point is not to strive in your own strength, but, like Paul, to press on to live increasingly more in Him, receiving the gifts of grace He has for us.

May you be encouraged to persevere in your journey of living in your identity in Christ.

I Live with Hope

*"May the God of hope fill you with all joy and peace in believing,
so that by the power of the Holy Spirit you may abound in hope."*
Romans 15:13 (ESV)

When you consecrated your life to Jesus, you became a new creature. As a result, the Spirit of God now lives inside you. All the facets of identity you have read about in the previous days are yours in Christ (along with many others found in Scripture). This enables you to have great hope.

Let's define our terms with this word, *hope*, however. Christ-centered hope is not merely a wish, like many people use the term. "I hope it doesn't rain today" is really a way of saying, "I wish it wouldn't rain today" or "It sure would be nice if it didn't rain today."

For the Christian, hope is founded on something solid—our loving God. Your hope is in the salvation offered by Jesus, which brings you new and eternal life. Often the world can make you feel like the ground is shifting under your feet. Your circumstances might not seem secure. But if you are in Christ, you have a firm foundation.

In Christ, you have a twofold hope: hope for today and hope for an eternity of joy in the presence of God.

Even so, you may struggle now and then to have hope. Many things in our world oppose hope in Christ. Romans 15:13 paints a picture of precious, good news: God is the one doing the heavy lifting. He is the one who provides hope. If you know Christ, the Holy Spirit is holding the hope for you—you do not have to hold onto hope in your own strength. That is very good news indeed.

In Christ and by the power of the Holy Spirit living within you, you can be full of assurance whatever you face. You are able to be filled with hope in Him.

Reflect: How would you rate your sense of hope in God? Does your life reflect hopefulness?

Loving God, empower me to press on into a life of abundant hope. Thank You that I can cry out to You for a more hopeful life today.

God's Word assures me I can abound in hope through the power of the Holy Spirit living in me. Therefore, I am hopeful.

DAY 23
I Live Expectantly

"Be silent before the LORD and wait expectantly for him; do not be agitated by one who prospers in his way, by the person who carries out evil plans."

Psalm 37:7 (CSB)

The word *expectant* is closely related to the word *hope*. In Christ, you can be hopeful. In Christ, you also can live expectantly, in an eager, anticipatory way.

The quality of what people expect can vary. Some people expect good things, while others expect the worst. Some people are characterized by what I would call the opposite of expectancy—apathy, disinterest, or indifference. Plenty of people live in that space.

As a new creature in Christ, you are no longer enslaved to an orphan spirit that would have you living in places of low expectations or no expectations. You can and should walk in a posture of hopeful expectation. The Father has good things in store for you; Christ assures your future.

Scripture reminds us that He is a good Father whose glory is revealed in the creation around us (Psalm 19). God is everywhere, surrounding us with His beauty, His mercy, His protection, and His care. And today's verse reminds you that you can wait expectantly for Him, even when circumstances around you look unfair or unjust.

The cares and burdens of this life can make you weary and worn down. But you do not have to make your home there. You can lift your eyes up and recall your help will come from the Lord who made heaven and earth (Psalm 121:2).

Even in the midst of hard things, the glory of God is still present. In every place, you can confidently expect His presence with you. Not only do you have this presence now, but in Christ, you have a glorious, eternal future.

You can wait expectantly for Him by the power of His Spirit living within you. May you walk with expectancy today and live with anticipation of His full redemption of all.

Reflect: How would you rate your sense of expecting good things from God? Do you live a life of confident expectancy?

Loving God, I receive the truth that I can expect good things from You, like mercy and eternal life. Help me to live expectantly today.

I can live in expectation of God's mercy, presence, and grace. I expect good things.

DAY 24
I Live Confidently

"I am confident of this, that the one who began a good work in
you will continue to complete it until the day of Jesus Christ."
Philippians 1:6 (NRSVUE)

Isn't confidence something you desire more of?

Today's verse reveals that Paul, the author of Philippians, had great confidence in God to finish the good work of salvation and sanctification He had begun in the believers in Philippi. What did Paul base his confidence on? The faithfulness of God.

Paul was no stranger to challenges and temptations, but he knew the prevailing power of Christ to meet him in his places of weakness (Romans 7:15-25). Based on his years of experiencing the faithful, perfecting work of Christ in his life, Paul was confident of God's faithfulness for others.

God's faithfulness should give you great confidence, too. This verse emphasizes the fact that God is at work in His children, bringing about their perfection. If you have surrendered yourself to Jesus, God is growing you, nurturing you, healing you, restoring you, and fully perfecting you until the day you see Jesus face to face.

So, your confidence does not have to be shaken when you make a mistake or when life does not go as you planned. God is still at work in you. He began a good work in you. He will be faithful to complete it.

Take a moment to consider the types of events or circumstances that shake your confidence.

Now think back over the characteristics of identity in Christ you have been meditating on for the past weeks. Isn't there something in your identity in Christ that would meet and conquer what shakes your confidence?

Even more, recall that, in Christ, your confidence does not rest on your own shoulders, but on His. He is continuing to complete the good work He began in you. He is not sitting back, keeping track of your shortcomings. He is at work making you perfect. What a confidence booster it is to realize this truth.

Reflect: What causes you to lack confidence? Do you place more confidence in yourself or in Christ?

Loving God, I receive the truth that I can be confident in You for all things. Help me to live in that confidence today.

God tells me He will complete the good work He has begun in me. I am confident in Christ.

DAY 25
I Live with Assurance

"And since we have a great high priest over the house of God, let us draw near to God with a sincere heart and with the full assurance that faith brings…"
Hebrews 10:21-22a (NIV)

I'm old enough to remember singing hymns in church every Sunday. One I have strong memories of is Fanny Crosby's *Blessed Assurance*. We sang it at many Wednesday-night suppers at the Baptist church of my childhood.

The first verse says: "Blessed assurance, Jesus is mine. Oh, what a foretaste of glory divine. Heir of salvation, purchase of God. Born of His Spirit, washed in His blood."[8]

This lyric, like our verse for today, tells us the source of all assurance: Jesus.

What are you assured of? According to Hebrews 10, the assurance for Jesus' present-day disciples is this: Christ Jesus has fully forgiven your sins, and He has perfected you. No wonder Fanny Crosby called it *blessed* assurance.

The hymn's first verse names four additional blessings you have in Christ: a glorious future; salvation; you are born of His Spirit; you are washed clean by Jesus' blood.

Scripture affirms all of these truths about your identity in Christ.

Do you struggle to remember how strongly you are assured of glorious relationship with God? Do you forget that you can draw near to Him without shame or fear? Rejoice! Your forgetfulness does not mean these realities aren't true.

The chorus of Crosby's hymn holds an additional clue for how to walk in your assurance. Twice the chorus repeats this line: "This is my story, this is my song, praising my Savior all the day long."

If you sing the hymn's three verses all the way through, you will assert a testimony of Christ in your life six times. Repetition of truth does something significant to your soul. So does focusing on Jesus in praise. Accept into your life the blessed assurance of identity in Christ. Make it your story. Make it your song.

Reflect: Do you find it easy or difficult to draw near to God in full assurance of Him welcoming you?

Loving God, thank You that, in Christ, I am assured that I am forgiven, that I can draw near to You, and that I have a glorious future. Help me to live in this assurance today.

I can draw near to God in full assurance of forgiveness. I am assured in Christ.

DAY 26
I Live with Strength

"You then, my child, be strengthened by the grace that is in Christ Jesus."

2 Timothy 2:1 (ESV)

One of the earliest songs I learned was *Jesus Loves Me*. From as far back as I can remember, the line that stood out to me is, "Little ones to Him belong; They are weak, but He is strong."

Since I was a little person when I learned the song, this line made me feel included. Safe. I could sense I wasn't quite big enough to fend for myself in a grown-up world. I'm really no different now.

Somehow as we grow up from childhood, we lose our ability to acknowledge and to be okay with our weakness. At the very least we go to a lot of trouble to disguise it. Weakness is preyed upon in our world. It is preached against in our world. The products and proclamations of our world are dedicated to propelling us to strength.

Despite all the messages we receive, the *Jesus Loves Me* lyrics are onto something profound and exhilarating. We are weak. Jesus is strong. The only path to true strength is by admitting our weakness and relying upon Him.

Today's verse shows the Bible exhorting you to strength. But it exhorts you to strength in the context of reliance upon God. You become strong through Him and His grace.

You are weak. You are frail. And that is okay. To pretend otherwise is exhausting.

When your identity is in Christ, your weakness becomes a pathway to the greatest, most comforting strength in all the Universe—the strength of God. As a child of the King, you have access to His strength, and you can live in reliance upon it.

The Bible exhorts you to live in that place: "Finally, be strong in the Lord and in the strength of His might" (Ephesians 6:10, NASB). May you walk in His strength today.

Reflect: How well do you experience a sense of strength in Christ? Are you more likely to rely on His strength or your own?

Loving God, thank You that I can be strong in Christ. Whether I am overconfident in myself or don't feel confident at all, bring me into alignment with Christ's strength today.

Regardless of the situation, I can rely on Christ's strength. I am strong in Christ.

I Live as One
Who Is Complete

"So you also are complete through your union with Christ, who is the head over every ruler and authority."

Colossians 2:10 (NLT)

The Greek word here translated as *complete* means "to make full, to fill, or to fill up." This verse has the sense of something being diffused throughout one's soul.[9] The perfection of Christ fills you to the brim. Through union with Christ, you are complete.

But oh, how challenging it can be to live in a sense of that completion.

A battle rages for your heart and your emotions. The enemy wants to obscure your perception of how truly complete and whole you are in Christ. He wants to blind you to your true identity, and consequently to keep you feeling as though you are deprived or lacking.

Look again, though, at how Jesus is described in the last seven words of this verse: *"the head over every ruler and authority."*

When Paul writes of rulers and authorities in the New Testament, he is not usually referring to world leaders or your boss. He is talking about agents of the unseen spiritual realm; demonic and evil powers opposed to God and His children.

But Jesus is head over all things. No authority anywhere on earth or in the spiritual realm is outside His control. The reason you can forget you are complete in Christ is that it is easy to forget the absolute authority of Christ. It is far too easy to believe distracting, accusing, or condemning voices coming at you from both within and without.

Union with Christ is the key to experiencing the completion He purchased for you on the cross. What a wondrous truth: Christ lives in you through the Holy Spirit. You are united with Him, and He perfects and completes you.

Reflect: What disrupts your sense of being fully united with Christ? Do you invite God to restore your union with Him in those places?

Loving God, I receive the truth that in union with Christ I am complete. Restore our union today from all the forces that seek to damage and drag me away from completion in Christ.

Christ's authority and rule triumph over all disruptions to union with Him. I am complete in Christ.

I Live Freely

"For freedom, Christ set us free. Stand firm, then, and don't submit again to a yoke of slavery…For you were called to be free, brothers and sisters; only don't use this freedom as an opportunity for the flesh…I say, then, walk by the Spirit and you will certainly not carry out the desire of the flesh."

Galatians 5:1, 13, 16 (CSB)

Over the past weeks, you have encountered much truth about your identity in Christ. Taking in and walking in these truths leads to tremendous freedom in Him.

We often perceive freedom as the ability to do whatever we want to do, whenever we want to do it. It is more accurate to describe that mindset as independence, and that point of view is a slippery slope leading to all sorts of self-absorption and selfishness. Our flesh longs for independence from anything confining or enslaving. So, let us be clear-eyed about the nature of Christian freedom.

Christian freedom is freedom from enslavement, but dependence on Christ is the only way this freedom is gained. We think of freedom and independence as synonyms. It is counterintuitive to speak of freedom and dependence in the same breath, but that is the way of Christ.

Paul describes this tension well in Galatians 5. He admonishes in verse 1 not to "submit again to a yoke of slavery" (ESV). What kind of slavery? The slavery of "old-man" thinking that focuses on your own works or effort for gaining identity instead of resting in the identity Christ has purchased for you. A great challenge of Christian discipleship is not submitting again to slavery.

In verses 13 and 16, Paul writes of the flesh. Everyone battles with desires to have true independence from not only others, but from God as well. It was precisely this human tendency that Satan exploited with Adam and Eve in the Garden. The enemy continues to woo toward independence while God is wooing to dependence upon Him, which leads to true freedom.

You can be tempted to lean on a self-help mindset instead of a Spirit-help mindset. Paul says if you walk with the Spirit, you will NOT carry out the desires of your flesh. This is huge. The one "job" you have is to be in step with the Spirit who tells you all the truths of Christ.

Freedom is yours in Christ, and it comes from dependence on His Spirit living within you. Keeping in step with the Spirit and cultivating this relationship is the most significant thing you will ever do. May you rely on the Spirit to guide you into the truths of your identity in Christ, to restore your union with Him daily, and to walk increasingly in the freedom Christ offers you.

Reflect: Do you enjoy freedom in Christ? What sorts of things try to enslave you to "old-man" thinking?

Loving God, help me receive the truth that I am free in Christ and can walk in freedom through dependence upon the Holy Spirit. Help me to live in this Spirit-dependent freedom today.

In Christ, I am free from striving to be loved or trying to earn my salvation. I am free to embrace the abundant life Christ has purchased for me.

SECTION FOUR
Declare Truth

These final entries offer a "next step" for embracing your identity in Christ, giving you an opportunity to personalize aspects of identity you most need to take into your daily life right now.

Days 29 and 30 invite you to reflect on the previous days of truth and give you a tool for taking a specific step toward walking boldly in the identity you have in Jesus.

The exercises found in the next two entries are also repeatable. Consider revisiting them on a regular basis—monthly or once a quarter. This tool helps cultivate timely and personalized reliance on God's truth about who you are in Him.

Below is a list of each of the twenty-eight topics you have read about. You will use this as part of the next exercises:

Day 1: Imago Dei
Day 2: Made with Purpose
Day 3: Challenged by a Liar
Day 4: Delivered and Transferred
Day 5: Debt Free
Day 6: New in Christ
Day 7: Perfected in Faith
Day 8: Alive
Day 9: Blameless
Day 10: Beloved
Day 11: Included
Day 12: Child
Day 13: Clothed
Day 14: Chosen
Day 15: Restored
Day 16: Rescued
Day 17: Redeemed
Day 18: Seen
Day 19: Known
Day 20: Accepted
Day 21: Friend
Day 22: I Live with Hope
Day 23: I Live Expectantly
Day 24: I Live Confidently
Day 25: I Live with Assurance
Day 26: I Live with Strength
Day 27: I Live as One Who Is Complete
Day 28: I Live Freely

Reflect on Truth

"Instead, his delight is in the LORD's instruction, and he
meditates on it day and night."

Psalm 1:2 (CSB)

Scripture often reminds us to reflect and meditate on God's truths. This is critically important when it comes to truth about your identity in Christ. Many, many things war against your belief and trust in what He says about you.

Today, take time to review and to reflect on the truths you have encountered in this devotion about who you are in Christ. Your goal is to zero in on two or three truths that "hit you where you live" right now. These steps will guide you gently back through the content:

1. Look at the list of each day's topics on the previous page. Set a timer for three minutes, and either make a separate list or circle ones that resonate with you. Don't overthink it. Simply let this step be a quick starting point.

2. Next, look at the Affirmations on pages 74-75. This lists the affirmations at the end of each of the 28 days. Read each one, aloud if possible. As you read, take note of what stands out. Pay attention to ones that express something you desire to have more of or to ones that you might struggle to believe about yourself. Mark those or write them on a separate piece of paper. This should generate a second list for you to consider.

3. Put your responses (or lists) from steps 1 and 2 side by side. Using the prayer below as a starting point, prayerfully review the lists, asking God to help you identify the top two or three topics that are for you to pay attention to right now. Especially pay attention to any topics that appeared in both steps.

4. Once you have identified your top two or three, turn back to those entries and re-read them. Take note of any truths you most want to hang onto. This step is also useful if you find yourself struggling to narrow down two or three truths to focus on.

You will take this information into a separate activity tomorrow.

Loving God, help me to identify the facets of my identity in Christ I need most right now in my life. Shine Your light on the specific truths You want me to embrace today. Guide me to see what You have for me in this season.

Dare to Declare

*"Since my youth, God, you have taught me, and to this day I
declare your marvelous deeds."*

Psalm 71:17 (NIV)

After yesterday, you should have a good idea of two or three truths the
Lord is guiding you to focus on. Today, you will craft a declaration of
those truths—a tool that will help you remind yourself of these truths
regularly.

What does it mean to declare? A contemporary dictionary will include
the idea of stating something emphatically. The Hebrew word
translated *declare* in our verse today is a verb that means "to be
conspicuous."[10] I like that idea—*declaring* as conspicuously stating
something. Oddly, it reminds me of the lyrics to the childhood chorus
"This Little Light of Mine." I recall as a child declaring loudly and
confidently in song that I was not going to hide my light under a
bushel.

The Bible talks about declaring truth in different settings, including in
corporate worship and to the rulers and powers of the unseen realm (2
Corinthians 10:3-6; Ephesians 3:10, 6:10-20). You will want to shine
the light of God's truth into your own heart as well.

In terms of your spiritual formation, immense value comes in
intentionally, conspicuously affirming what God says is true, *whether or
not your feelings at the moment line up with that truth*. You are to walk by

faith, not by sight (2 Corinthians 5:7). Affirming truth is a way of bolstering your faith, especially at times you cannot seem to see or feel truth experientially.

Below are steps for creating a declaration that is personal to you and your needs. Read all the steps to get ideas before you get to work. Next, you may want to take notes as you go back through each step. Then come back and write a final version.

There is not one "right" format for this, though I suggest a couple of options below. Sometimes I create a paragraph. Other times I only make a list of a few sentences. If you don't feel terribly creative, that is okay! You can also choose a Scripture or two and make those your declarations. I offer a sample on the next page.

1. If you have not identified two to three truths yet, go back to yesterday's exercises and dial that in. Ask the Holy Spirit to lead you.

2. Go to the devotional entry related to each truth you have chosen to focus on. Write out the verse at the top of that page, as well as the affirmation at the bottom of the page. Spend time meditating on them, noting any insights that emerge.

3. Decide if you want to write a declaration about just one truth or a declaration that includes all the ones you have selected. Either is fine. What do you sense the Lord pointing to?

4. For a simple declaration of one truth, you can let the affirmation and verse be your entire declaration. If you are using two or three topics, combine those verses and affirmations together.

5. You can add personalization by including ideas or phrases from the Bible verse or from the devotional entry. You can also rephrase them to reflect what your heart most needs to be reminded of.

6. If you want to take it a step further, look at other verses about the topic you are writing a declaration about. Find additional verses using a concordance or cross reference tool in your Bible or online.

7. That's it! Write it out. You can write it on a sticky note, type it into a document to print, or create it into a decorative page to frame. The important thing is to put it where you can see it and repeat it aloud each day until you find yourself confidently embracing this facet of your identity in Christ.

Here is a declaration I wrote at a time I needed God to remind me of my belovedness. You might recognize I borrowed language both from Bible verses and from lyrics of Scripture-based praise songs.

I am deeply loved and cherished by God.
He lives within me and delights in me.
He holds me fast. He is faithful. I am surrounded by His love, His holy jealousy,
and His angel armies.
He is for me. He fights for me; I need only be still.

May you find this practice to increase your confidence in God and His truth about you.

Congratulations!

You have finished this 30-day journey of discovery about the truth of your identity in Christ. I pray it has been a blessing that has encouraged your heart. He loves you so much.

Here are some next steps to take to stay connected to the truths you've found here:

- Make a copy of the declaration you wrote on Day 30 and post it somewhere you can see it and proclaim it aloud each day.

- Schedule a time on your calendar one month from now to revisit Days 29 and 30 from this journey and repeat the process of identifying truths you most need to lean into about your identity in Christ.

- Invite a friend (or a group of friends) to get a copy of the book and work through it as a means of accountability and staying in the Word within a community.

- If this book blessed you and made a positive impact on your relationship with Christ, would you take a minute to post a review of it on Amazon? Each review of this book helps reach more people with the message of God's deep love.

- Visit elizabethrenicks.com to find more resources to empower and encourage your journey with God and to help you know more of Him.

Affirmations of Truth About Who I Am in Christ

Day 1: God is the foundation of my identity; therefore, I am valuable and beloved.

Day 2: God made me with a unique purpose, and He is with me in living it out.

Day 3: I will face opposition in living as a beloved child of God, but in Christ, I have victory over those challenges.

Day 4: As a Christian, I no longer live in the domain of darkness. Christ has transferred me into the realm of light.

Day 5: Jesus has erased all my debts. I am debt free in God's eyes.

Day 6: Christ has made me new, and I can learn to walk in that newness with His faithful care.

Day 7: I am not alone walking out my faith. Jesus begins and completes it. I can rely on His faithfulness to grow me into what He has planned for me.

Day 8: I can choose to believe I am alive in Christ and dead to any sin that tries to dull my life in Him.

Day 9: In Christ, I am blameless before God. I can reject condemnation.

Day 10: I am God's beloved. He delights in me.

Day 11: I am never alone because Christ includes me. When I feel alone, I can cry out to God to remind me I am included.

Day 12: I am a child of God, which means I belong to the most royal ruling family of all time.

Day 13: I am clothed in royal robes of righteousness. I can reject accusations and shame because of what Jesus has done for me.

Day 14: I am chosen by God. He sees me, and He chooses me.

Day 15: In Christ, I am restored to God, and He is restoring all the worn-out things in my soul.

Day 16: I have been rescued by a responsive and loving God. He releases me from all snares.

Day 17: I am redeemed. Jesus Christ has paid the ransom for all things attempting to take me hostage.

Day 18: I am seen by the great, merciful, and compassionate God who created all things.

Day 19: I am fully known by a compassionate and merciful God who loves me.

Day 20: Regardless of my circumstances, I am accepted—highly favored—by Christ at all times.

Day 21: I am a friend of God. I can have an intimate relationship with Him.

Day 22: God's Word assures me I can abound in hope through the power of the Holy Spirit living in me. Therefore, I am hopeful.

Day 23: I can live in expectation of God's mercy, presence, and grace. I expect good things.

Day 24: God tells me He will complete the good work He has begun in me. I am confident in Christ.

Day 25: I can draw near to God in full assurance of forgiveness. I am assured in Christ.

Day 26: Regardless of the situation, I can rely on Christ's strength. I am strong in Christ.

Day 27: Christ's authority and rule triumph over all disruptions to union with Him. I am complete in Christ.

Day 28: In Christ, I am free from the burden of striving to be loved or trying to earn my salvation. I am free to embrace the abundant life Christ has purchased for me.

Endnotes

[1] "The Purpose Driven Life." *Wikipedia*, Wikimedia Foundation, 8 Aug. 2025, en.wikipedia.org/wiki/The_Purpose_Driven_Life.

[2] "G5498 - Cheirographon - Strong's Greek Lexicon (KJV)." *Blue Letter Bible*, www.blueletterbible.org/lexicon/g5498/kjv/tr/0-1/.

[3] "*Oxford English Dictionary,* s.v. "blameless." apps.apple.com/us/oxford-dictionary/id978674211.

[4] "G410 - Anegklētos - Strong's Greek Lexicon (ESV)." *Blue Letter Bible*, www.blueletterbible.org/lexicon/g410/kjv/tr/0-1/.

[5] "G629 - Apolytrōsis - Strong's Greek Lexicon (KJV)." *Blue Letter Bible*, www.blueletterbible.org/lexicon/g629/kjv/tr/0-1/.

[6] Author: Fanny Crosby Pseudonymns: A.V., Mrs. A. E. Andrews. "Redeemed, How I Love to Proclaim It!" *Hymnary.Org*, hymnary.org/text/redeemed_how_i_love_to_proclaim_it.

[7] "G5487 - Charitoō - Strong's Greek Lexicon (KJV)." *Blue Letter Bible*, www.blueletterbible.org/lexicon/g5487/kjv/tr/0-1/.

[8] Author: Fanny Crosby Pseudonymns: A.V., Mrs. A. E. Andrews. "Blessed Assurance." *Hymnary.Org*, hymnary.org/text/blessed_assurance_jesus_is_mine.

[9] "G4137 - Plēroō - Strong's Greek Lexicon (KJV)." *Blue Letter Bible*, www.blueletterbible.org/lexicon/g4137/kjv/tr/0-1/.

[10] "H5046 - Nāḡaḏ - Strong's Hebrew Lexicon (KJV)." *Blue Letter Bible*, www.blueletterbible.org/lexicon/h5046/kjv/wlc/0-1/.

About the Author

Elizabeth Renicks is a Bible teacher, writer, and speaker. More than that, she is a woman who knows the beauty of discovering real intimacy with God after exhausting years of striving in her own strength. With warmth, wisdom, and a deep love for Scripture, she equips women to foster a restful, restorative relationship with Christ.

A truth teller who infuses every message with encouragement and hope, she offers the wisdom and experience of decades as a serious student of God's Word. With more than 30 years' experience teaching, writing, and speaking, Elizabeth is a trusted resource for insight and encouragement.

She is the author of *Missio Dei: Joining God on the Adventure of a Lifetime,* a high school Bible course that has been used by Christian schools around the globe. She is also a contributor to the Guideposts anthologies *Wrapped in His Protection: True Stories of Everyday Miracles* and *Living the Word: Reflections on Scripture's Most Beloved Passages.* She is also a contributor to the devotional *God With Us, Immanuel: An Advent Devotional Through the Lineage of Christ.*

Elizabeth lives in Alabama with her husband and their two sons. An avid reader and life-long learner, she ministers through teaching and discipleship in her church and local homeschool community. Find her at elizabethrenicks.com.

Other Books
by Elizabeth Renicks

You Have an Invitation to Return and Rest in God

Feeling weary or spiritually stuck? I've been there. God used a passage in Isaiah 30 to redirect my focus and increase my trust in Him. I'm so thrilled to share what I've learned in the Bible study *Return and Rest: A Study in Isaiah 30.* In this six-week study you'll uncover God's timeless invitation to stop striving and find strength in Him, guiding you to rest in His presence, renew your trust, and rediscover the abundant life He promises.

Find your copy of *Return and Rest* on Amazon and begin your journey to deeper intimacy with God today.

Continue Your Journey of Flourishing in Faith

Fully Known, Fully Loved: A 30-Day Journey of Your Identity in Christ is just the beginning. This devotional is the first in my **Flourishing in Faith** series—resources designed to help you live more fully in intimacy with God by embracing His truth, resting in His love, and walking in freedom.

Each new devotional in this series will explore another foundational truth of the Christian life—helping you grow in grace, trust, and joy as you discover more of Him.

Sign up at this QR code to be the first to know when the next devotional releases, and to receive encouragement and tools to help you flourish in your faith.

What Could Your Life Look Like with More of Him?

Twice a month, I send grace-filled encouragement straight to your inbox to help you slow down and reconnect with God.

The *More of Him* newsletter includes:

- Encouragement to quiet the noise and hear God's voice

- Simple reminders of truth, identity, and grace

- Scripture-based prompts to keep you grounded and growing

Subscribe below and let's walk toward *more of Him*—together.

THANK YOU GIFT: A free PDF copy of a 10-day devotional: Truths About God's Guidance

ELIZABETH RENICKS

Find even more resources for increasing your intimacy with Him at www.elizabethrenicks.com